Figs and Promises

They shall all sit under their own vines,
under their own fig trees, undisturbed;
for the Lord of hosts has spoken.
Micah 4:4

More Poems and Paintings

Written by Karen Rhodes-Ochoa

ISBN 979-8-218-91807-1

karenro18@gmail.com

Edited by Nathaniel Lee Hansen,
nlhwritingservices.com

Cover design by Sydney Grace Weeks

Printed by Lulu Press, Inc.

To David, my husband,
a gift of grace in my life,
whose constant love has been a shelter,
and whose encouragement made space
for these words and images to grow.

No great thing is created suddenly, any more than a bunch of grapes or a fig. If you tell me that you desire a fig, I answer you that there must be time. Let it first blossom, then bear fruit, then ripen.

Epictetus, *Discourses* 1.15.7

Table of Contents

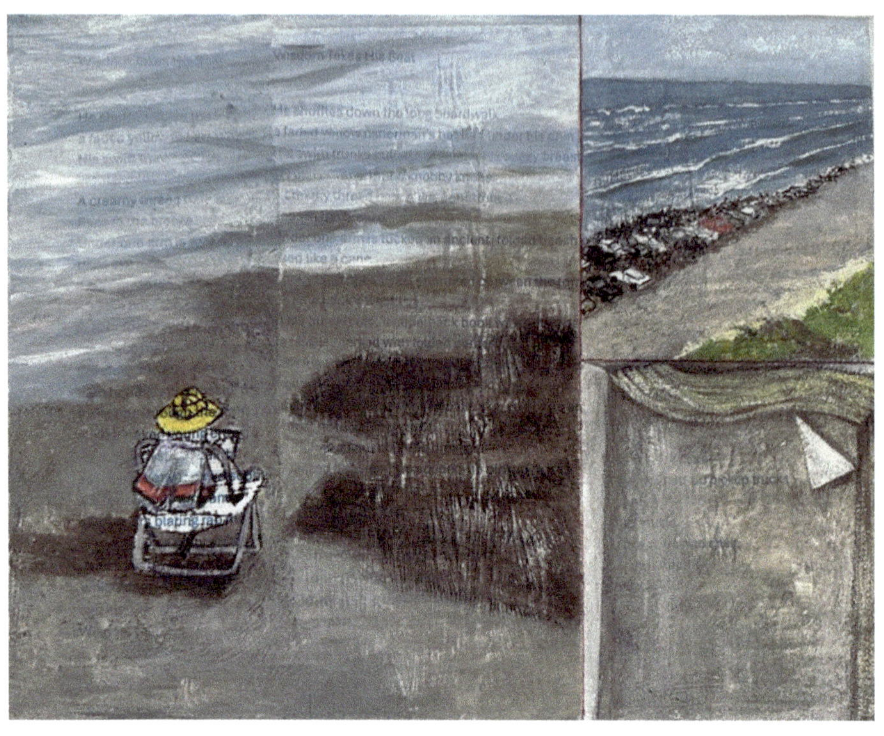

Wisdom Takes His Seat

He shuffles down the boardwalk,
a faded yellow fisherman's hat
tied under his chin.
Swim trunks high under saggy breasts
cover arthritic knobby knees.

A creamy thread-bare shirt
—unbuttoned—flaps in the breeze.
An ancient, folded beach chair
his make-do cane.

An old striped towel crammed
between the torn seat,
and the back's webbing.
In his other hand, a brittle paperback
marked with folded corners.

Carefully through the loose sand,
he threads a snarl
of cars, trucks, golf carts,
almost-naked young crowd.

He claims a spot near the breakers
squeezed between two souped-up trucks
with enormous tires, open doors blasting rap.

He unfolds his rusty chair,
places his towel over the straps
that dangle onto the sand,
and slowly lowers himself—

Wisdom takes his seat.

Proverbs 9

Two women stand in doorways
and call to all who pass their way,
Join me at my table
for a magnificent buffet.

Wisdom has built her home,
seven pillars under a dome.
Come all who are able,
to friends of God, I say shalom!

Folly has her abode
the height of the city's main road.
Calling the unstable,
on the simple her tricks bestowed.

Wisdom's guests are to first forsake
foolishness before they partake
wine, meat at her table
to live in wisdom, wide awake!

Folly serves what appears sweet—
stolen bread, water of deceit.
Her offers are but a fable,
her guests stay in a tomb—hell's heat!

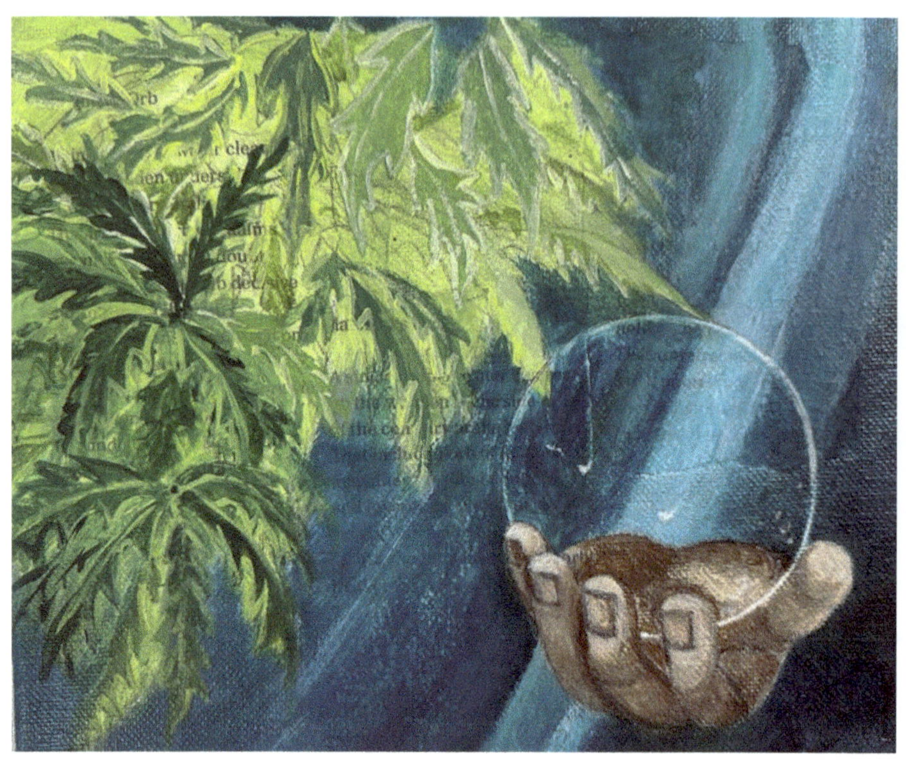

da Vinci's Orb

A drop of water cleaves
to the wooden underside
of the contrary aralia leaf —
that included orb of qualms
magnifies the dim of doubt
and inverts the plumb decisive
side of reconciliation.

Unlike the translucent royal orb
held in the palm of Christ —
that unrefracted Light of forgiveness
hung upon the wooden cross —
His undistorted robe of truth
remains divinely visible.

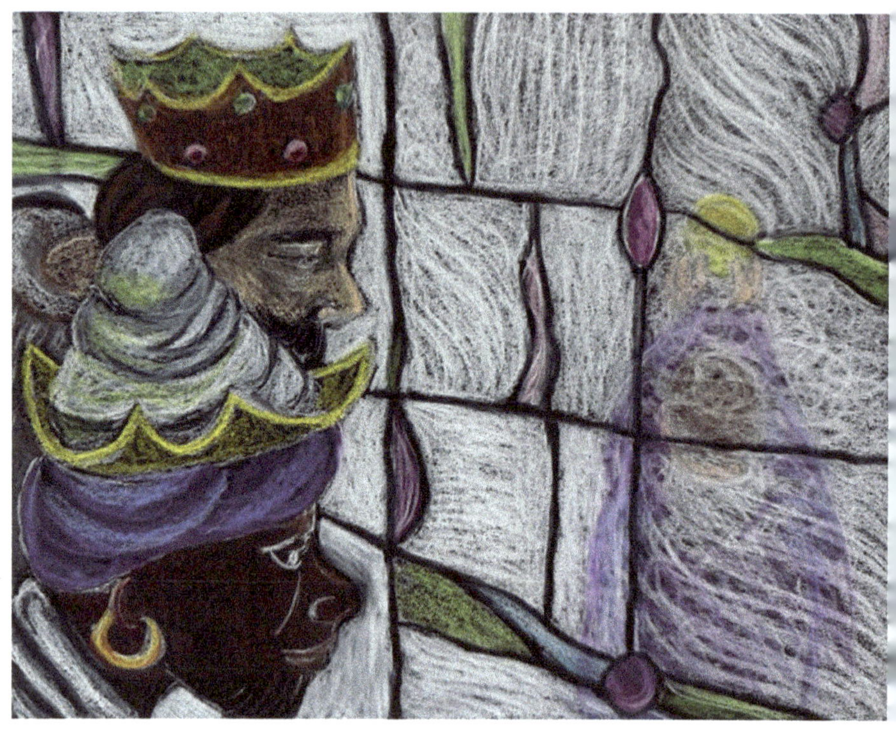

Magi of St. Albert

Traveling the way of wonder
bearing their precious gifts — precious too,
themselves —
carried in crates over the sea's rough line
packed secure in straw of advent waiting.

Through the pastoral hill country — onward
keeping pace with the strange star that foretells
with a bright unmistakable sign
the savior child's birth — The Cosmic King.

Finally freed from sealed-jeweled caskets
Caspar and Balthasar kneel in the not-yet —
still seeking to worship the Advocate,
at the close their quest — their faces pressed

against the foggy opaque-glass chantry
obscuring what they cannot, but long to see
that astounding moment of the epiclesis
promised to them — and to all — in Genesis.

The Many Baptisms of Agnes

Agnes joyfully submits
to the waters of suffering
a ternary of pouring
to Christ her heart commits.

Held in sentimental arms
over a ceramic wash bowl
Agnes receives blessings untold
oil, water protect her from harm.

She dresses in white tulle
upon refusing a suitor
whose father persecutes her—
strips and drags her to a brothel.

Her virginal white dress unfastened
upon accepting the anointing,
the wind of the Spirit outpointing
Agnes' pure soul impassioned.

Jesus—her spouse and lover—
heard, and answered her fervent prayer.
Agnes grew long rivers of hair
her nakedness, shame to cover.

Marked with an indelible seal
tributaries of unifying power,
Agnes strengthened for her coming hour
her innocence tested by searing ordeal.

Three fiery guardian angels
held a sword of obscuring light
protected Agnes from her cruel plight—
the base groping eyes of royals.

She is the water which douses flames.
Her face shimmers with light divine.
Agnes' uncharred chastity a sign
a perfect love which heaven proclaims.

A companion of the Lamb,
fearless under the garroter's sword
Her Christ and Savior Agnes adored.
Her courage as fragrant as balsam.

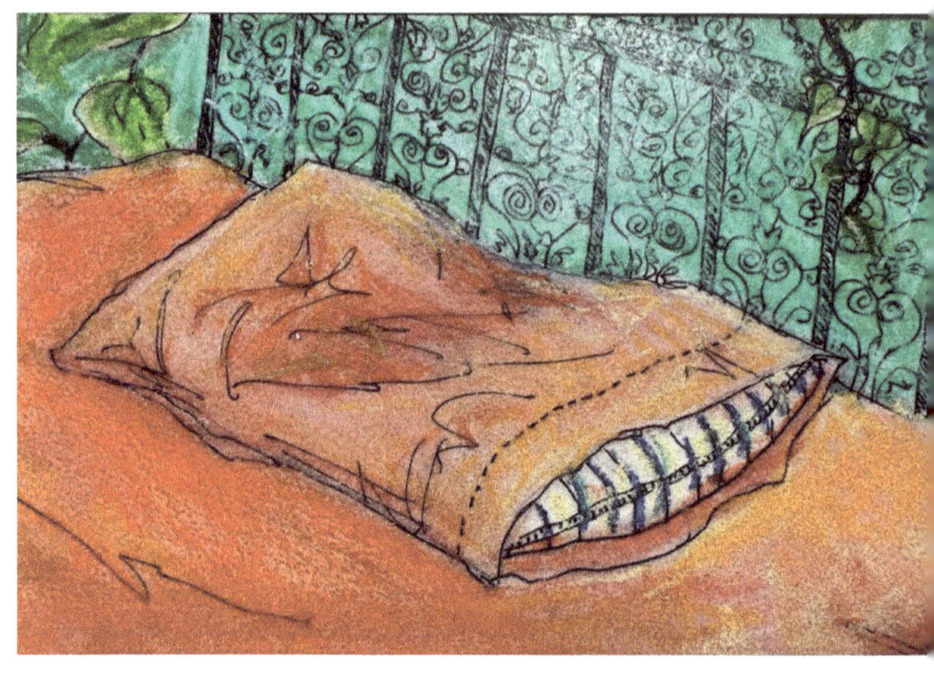

Sweet potato blues

Craving you,
I've got sweet potato blues.
Plant your head,
candied dreams in the night.
Before you close your eyes
and drift off,
burrow your hands beneath the cool pillow,
grasp the treasure I buried there,
a souvenir of our season together.
But I forgot to tell you
no sweet gift mine.

Sweet potato blues. . .
Sweet potato blues. . .
Sweet potato blues.

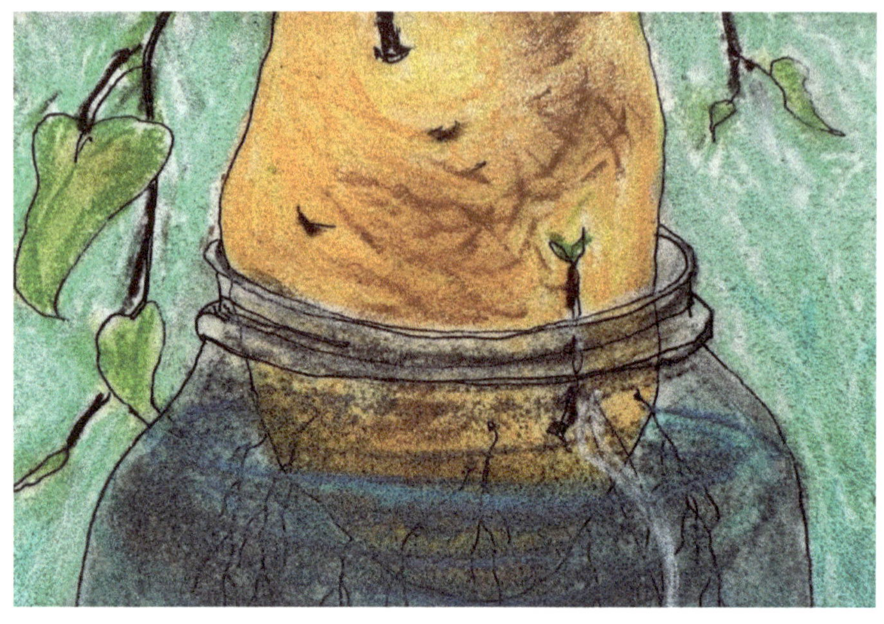

I sift through soft clumps
stored under fluorescent light
examining eyes for potential roots.
Carefully digging,
picking the perfect potato.
I store it in the cart.

Sweet potato blues. . .
Sweet potato blues. . .
Sweet potato blues.

Crammed into an old mason jar
filled with water
perched on the windowsill
gathering morning light,
it cowers.
No sprout,
no tiny fibers,
no fleshy tap.

Sweet potato blues. . .
Sweet potato blues. . .
Sweet potato blues.

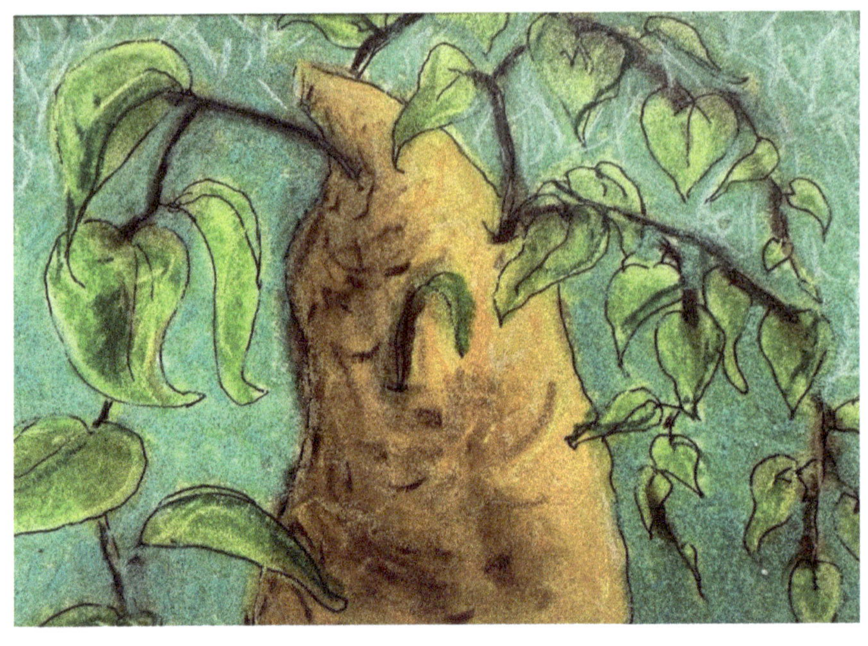

Infertile friendships end
in stagnant misunderstanding.
Why does your potato sprout
verdant hearts
while mine lay fallow?

Sweet potato blues. . .
Sweet potato blues. . .
Sweet potato blues.

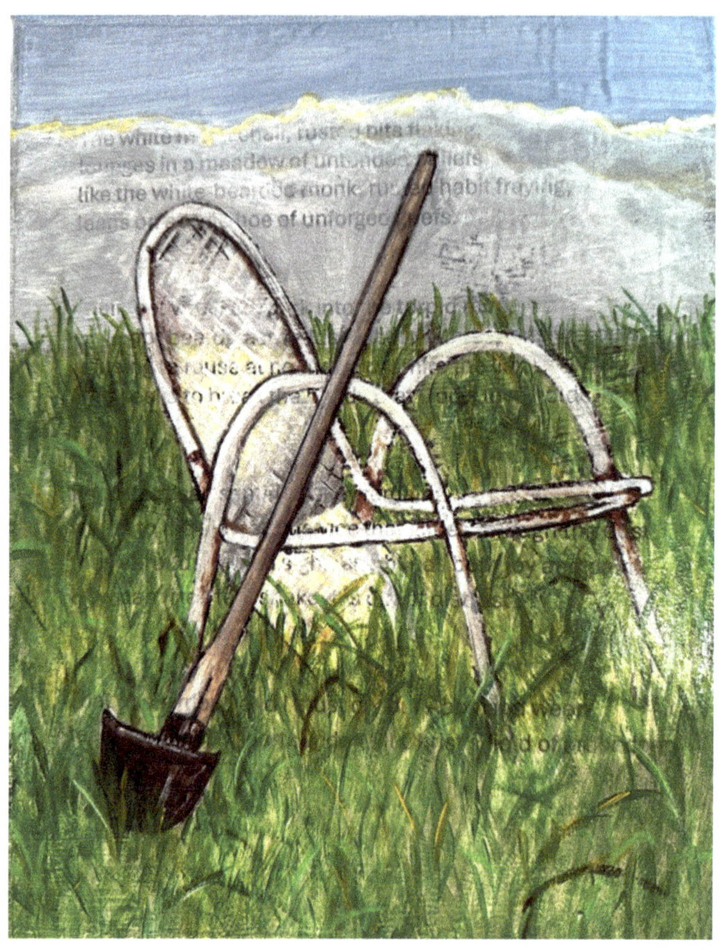

Acedia

The white metal chair, rusted bits flaking,
lounges in a meadow of untended beliefs
like the white-bearded monk, rusted habit fraying,
leans on an idle hoe of unforged griefs.

Their feet wrecked, dark in the torpid mire,
unkempt beardgrass holds fast their unresponsive
souls
refusing to rouse at noonday, or smite the liar
who seeks to break the bonds that God's love
holds.

Persistent sad sentinels they remain;
wards to the slow subtle vice that glides through
the dust
then shrouds sacred sight, and blinds both joy and
pain.
How can fixed feet shake this dirt of distrust?

That chair, monk and I must cry out *Abba* and
weep
tears that heave hearts wide – plow Christ's field
of ardor deep.

A Bare Season

Lukewarmness settles
over my chilled soul —
a snow-heavy cloud.

Grayness overcasts
every intention
with laden doubt —
freezes every hope.

Icy complacency
wraps around my mind
penetrating glutted motives —
faltering goodness.

Winter is a bare season —
shivering in anticipation
of a thawed faith.

Persistent

Elm—out of season
gold leaves in soul of winter
light yellow miracle.

Elm—out of season
gold leaves in drab of winter
blazing oriflammes.

Elm—out of season
gold leaves in gelid winter
bright consolation.

The Architecture of Bedlam

quickly becomes a fire hazard —
a peril to the soul, unless there's some
tackling the unholy mess gathered
atop the vena cava bureau —

those piles of coats yelling with impatience,
a bunch of unlabeled keys unlocking sorrow,
heaps of lonely socks of complacence.

And there, stuffed in the atrium
are backpacks filled with scarred childhood hurts,
enough boxes of doubts to fill a stadium,
and tubs of venial disconcerts last resorts.

In the ventricle's basement
a tangled mess — yarns of false beliefs,
twisted threads of unworthiness,
knots of *too late*, snarls of regrets and griefs.

Work upwards, sort through buckets of strife,
order boxes of trespasses, tidy crates of vice,
each part fitted together, compacted and proper
under the Master mover, Christ.

Lenten Observance

Spring, with sap — swollen
anticipations arise
pregnant clouds roll in.

*

Distant thunder claps
the rhythm — new beginnings
joy returns, perhaps.

*

Budding limbs sway, dance
a choreography of grace —
as the gray sky chants.

*

Descending square notes,
dun tones composed by the storm
considered spring hopes.

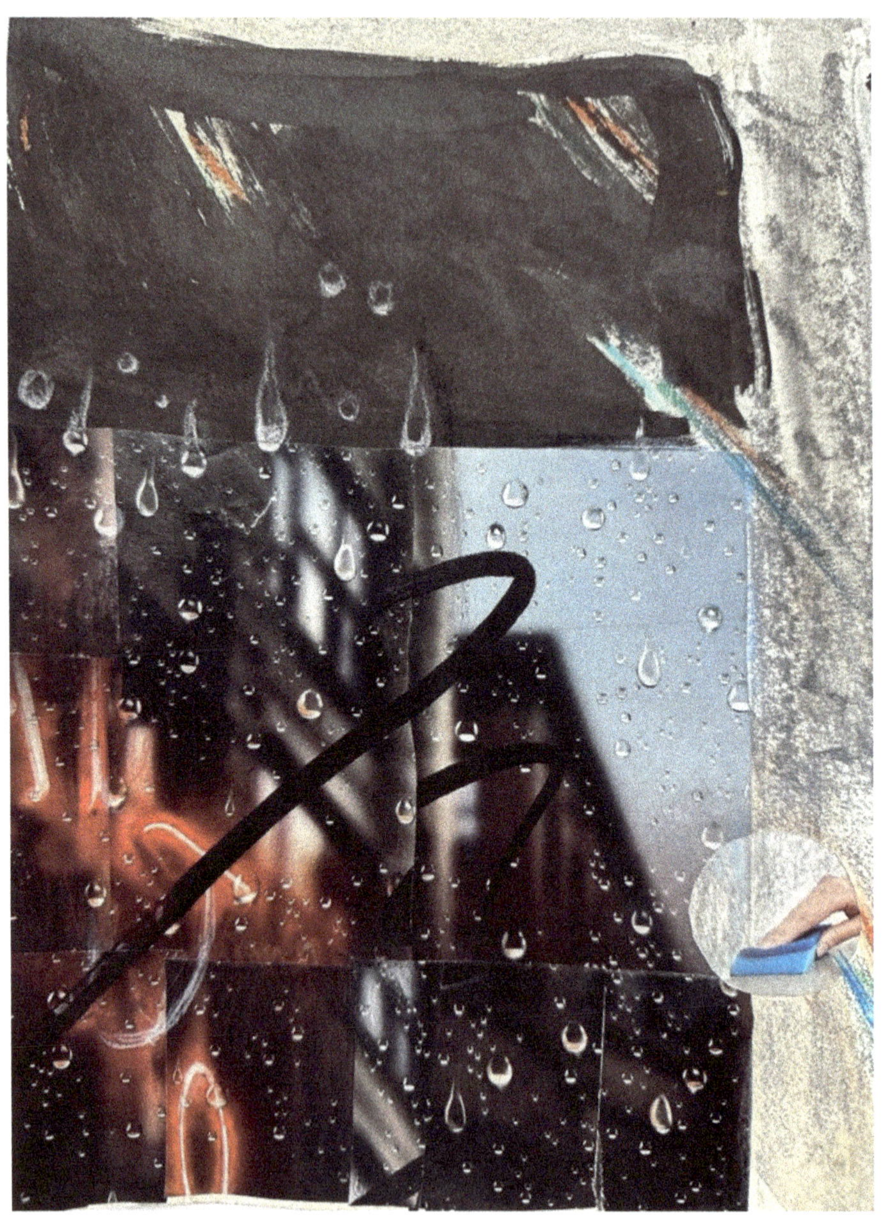

Confession

Smears of sin swish and careen,
wipe across my scummy soul.
The priest's Windexed prayers clean
smears of sin swish and careen
but squeaky clear grace foreseen
scrubbed ablution can't annul
smears of sin swish and careen
wipe across my scummy soul.

Glide low again

Perseids' peak predicted
comets *pick, pluck, plunk,*
in colorful icy streaks
across the moonless midnight sky
leaving persistent trains
long lacy showers of gold.
So near, singing low.

I am a Lake

— not restless as the sea,
but bound by particular borders
granting faithful reflection
and the reward of tranquility.

—not churning sand and foam,
but lucid crystal, transparent thought
that grants quiet integrity,
revealing the richness of my benthic zone.

— not windblown wild waves,
but gentle lapping swells
that grant sovereign sobriety
and a stout strength that saves.

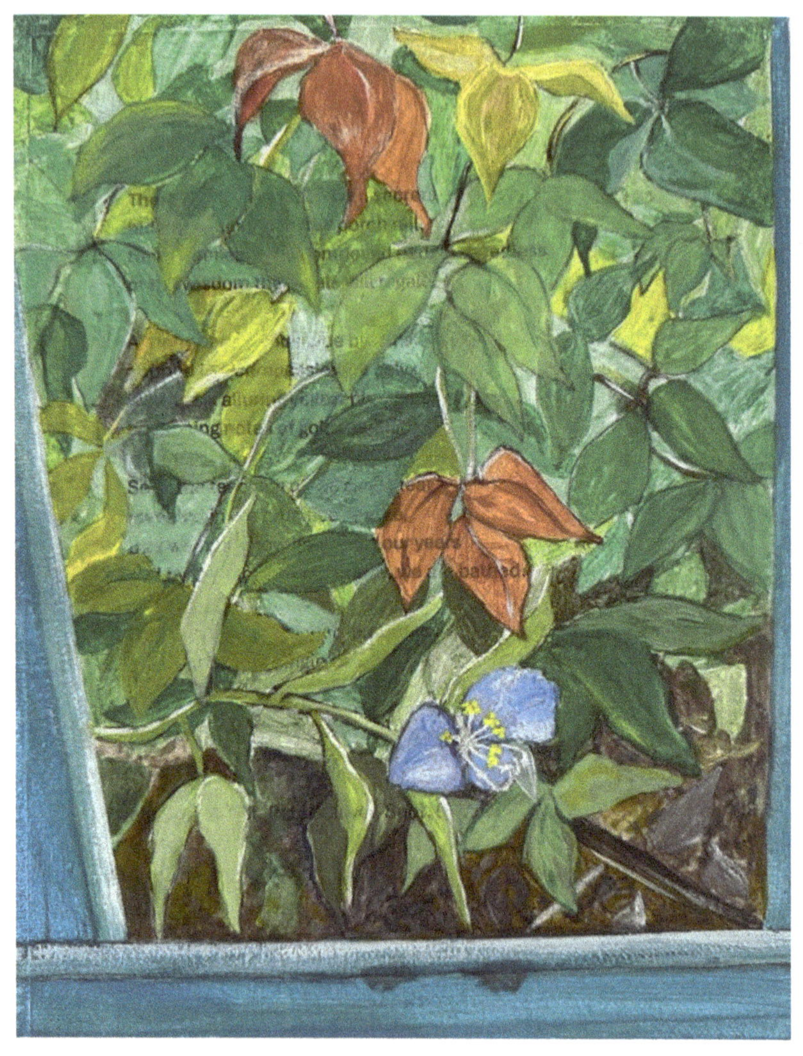

Tears of Blue

There are flowers laden with secrets
hidden under the sturdy porch rail,
tucked beneath the composed hedge — heedless
of the petal's wisdom regaled.

A trinity of righteous blue blooms
cupped in a compassionate calyx,
waving six alluring yellow plumes
beckoning notes of gold metallic.

Seek the teaching of the single tear
revealed in the crucified spathe,
that we may know how short our years
and with a drop of His blood we are bathed.

This ephemeral insight is on display
only just for one single day.

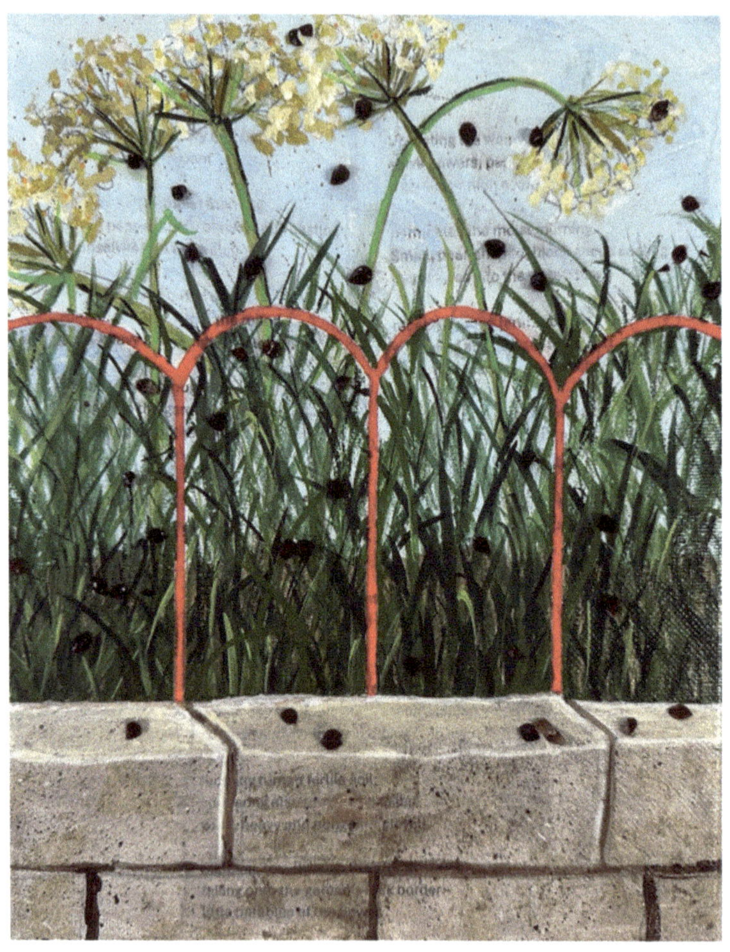

Little Parables

Uprooting the weary spent
chive flowers, papery and bent —
a garlicky-onion scent

permeates the moist morning.
Small, pear-shaped, black seeds casting
themselves into the welcoming

recently turned fertile soil;
scattering also toward the roiled
wind, heavy and pungent — cloyed.

Slipping, too, through the arbor,
falling onto the garden's rock border —
little parables of the Sower.

Do my meager considered deeds
produce growth, luscious green
abundant new leaves?

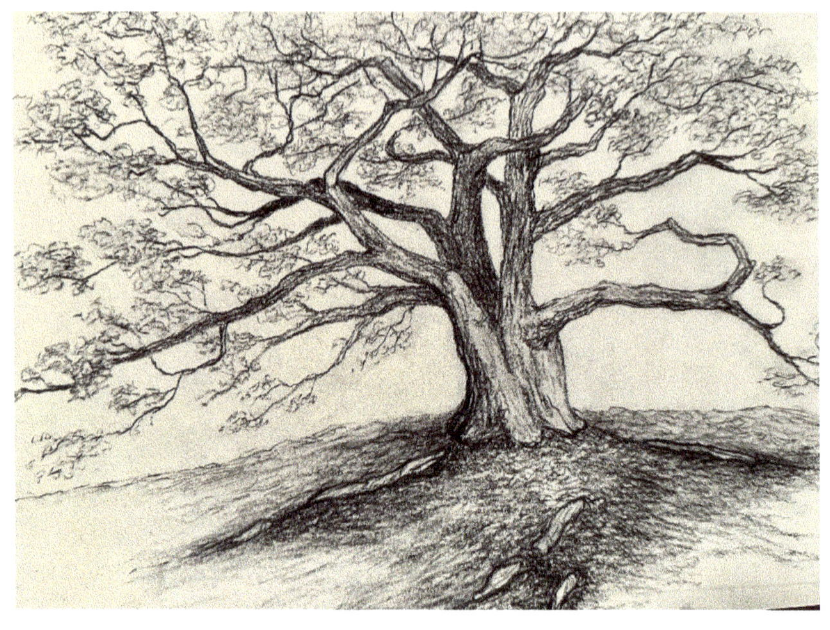

My Granddaughters Named It Anselm

The escarpment oak's wise canopy
guards our summer picnics.
Its short stout trunk
branches
in seven directions –
sacramentals of protection.

Twisted, gnarled limbs
curve, fashioning ribs
which endure
– possessing patience –
they bow in humility.

Its tangled roots grow
above imperfect soil –
wooden waves strike
your feet,
an angel's hand must
keep
you from stumbling.

Tardy deciduous shedding,
the verdant vesture

is exchanged every spring.
Tender new growth
a larval host
to mournful
Dusky Wings.

Celadon leaves emerge.
Drooping catkins
coat cars, roofs,
and hair
with yellow-green dust –
seven sneezes a sign of new life.

Its brown fusiform acorns –
gathered clusters
of faith.
They seek
to *be called*
oaks of righteousness,
the planting of the Lord,
to display his glory.

Willing to Become

Prostrate I lay down
ego's trowel, concreted sins –
my heart is like wax.

*

God extirpates
the tyranny of hurry –
He breaks all my bones.

*

Noble are my wounds –
they lead to a slower pace,
the gift of stillness.

*

A lifetime of wounds
surrendered in divine hope
bound with faithful gauze.

*

God, in His frailty,
willing to become enfleshed
and suffer with me.

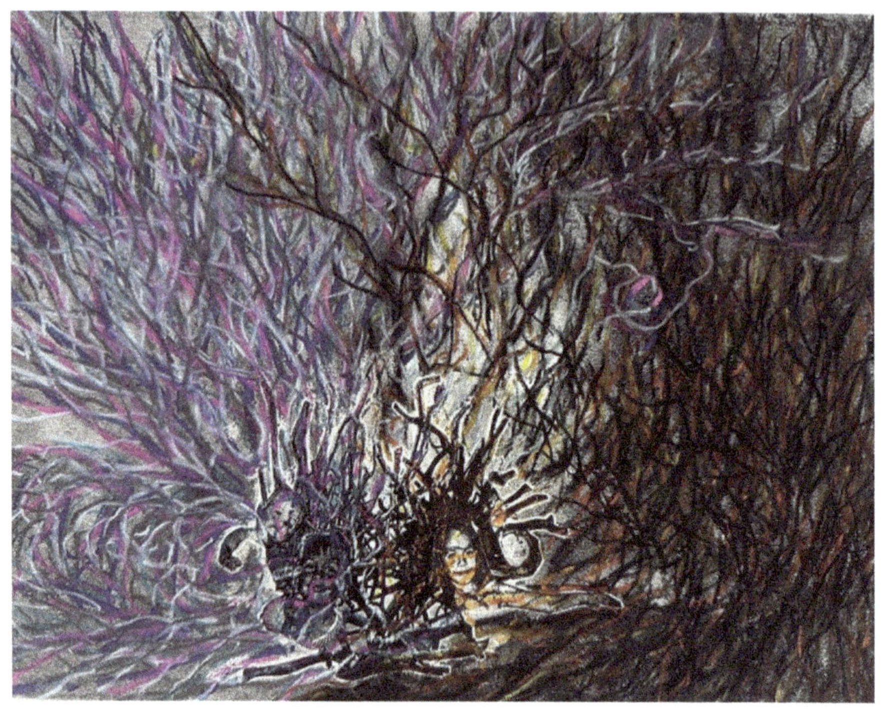

A Thistle Tumbling

Arising with the lengthening days of early summer
and thriving in the desolate-disturbed humble oil fields,
a ruderal weed fruits with girly light-pink blooms.
The thistle mutates from a budding-tender erect seedling
into a mangled callow-clump of branches,
a shocking tangle of sullen-scratchy spines
and needle-sharp leaves tipped with flaming crystals.
By the time shorter days and cooler nights arrive,
the morass of stems has dried
and become a brittle orb, woven with fibrous curses,
which waits in the uncomfortable arid silence
while a restless abscission weakens
the trunk and root's embrace.
They break apart as the winter winds,
brutal and intense, lift the round rolling remnant
sending it tumbling, tumbling, tumbling,
spreading new life over vast distances.
My God, make them like tumbleweed.

God, where were You?

My stuffing fingers singed
by branded allurements —
baited searing lies
of gratification —

My lacerated heart imbrued
by whips of birched remorse —
lashed cutting words
of torment —

My marred eyes distracted
by elusive glittering —
faraway fares
of solace —

My gnarled hands twisted
by the grasp of anxious cravings —
a begging breviary —
You were there.

God’s Heart

God’s heart breaks with the dark
lies dropping from parched tongues —
no grain of truth, such twisted hope
that splits hypocrisy’s hairs.

God’s heart heals broken fates,
every drowned sorrow —
wounds rubbed with salt of dashed hopes,
the hairy scalps who walk in sin.

God’s heart holds all the stars,
every drop in the sea,
grain of sand, each feather of hope,
even all the hairs on our heads.

Tillage of God

Pulling hard the paddle hoe
with all my might — yet still
unable to plow and harrow
weedy resentments — self-will
tightly attached to the roots
of my virtue — eel-like
nematodes infest the good fruits
cause blooms to wither — despite
my effort to till soiled fields.
Turn to the gardener, trust —
only His shovel of grace yields
holy roots — hint of harvest.

John 1: 37-41

Cerulean heavens ask me,
What is it that you seek?
I shrug — stutter — blunderingly,
unable yet to speak.

I gaze up — hesitant — inquire,
Where, Lord, are you staying?
Blue firmaments turning, reply,
Come — see the star raising —
only He can satisfy.

Daily Readings

The wind of wisdom
on the move – howls through the streets.
Gusts of wise words.

*

Praise born from His love
difficult and exhausting –
yet a sacred *Amen*.

*

Ability to see
with eyes of bees, wheat, oil –
Come Divine Wisdom!

*

Hold God's gifts gently
as the leaves fall, birds migrate
our hearts must let go.

Redeemed

The herd of deer — all women —
heads down — saunter through the yard
gossiping between pulled-bitten
nibbles of greensward.

All that moves and breathes in
the field belongs to me.

The weight of their words — nimble
bantered — tossed indifferently
in the patch of flowers purple
shamed the petals with effrontery.

I weep for children of Rachel —
even stones cry out.

Let the Lord's redeemed say so —
turn their hearts from conceit to meek
like a nipped blossom restored knows
pure new growth faith seeks.

Light that dwells in meadows —
hearts that flower revived.

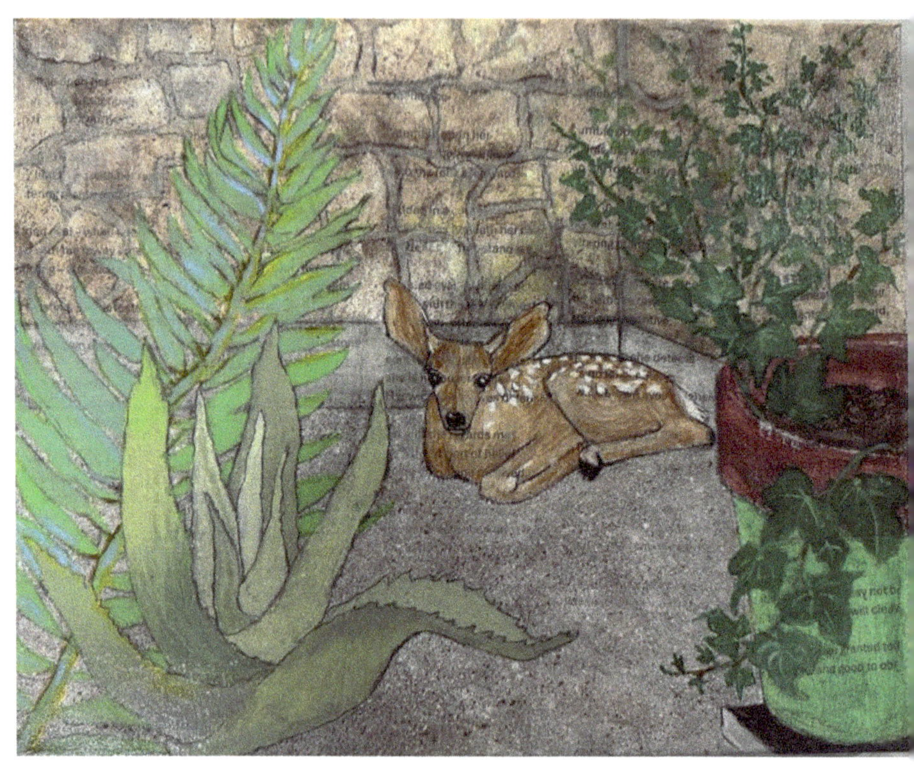

Obedience

I stumble upon her
as I drag the water hose
onto the rock courtyard.

Hidden in a corner,
lanky limbs beneath her nose.
Sheltering plants stand guard.

A curled oval — white specks
blend with the tawny limestone.
Unstirring — attentive,

ears twisting, she detects
she is no longer alone.
Her wide brown eyes defensive —

yet still she regards me
with the import of respect
in the command received.

Patience is her decree:
Mother's absence is not neglect.
So, to this rock she will cleave.

A blessed refuge granted today
for it is right and good to obey.

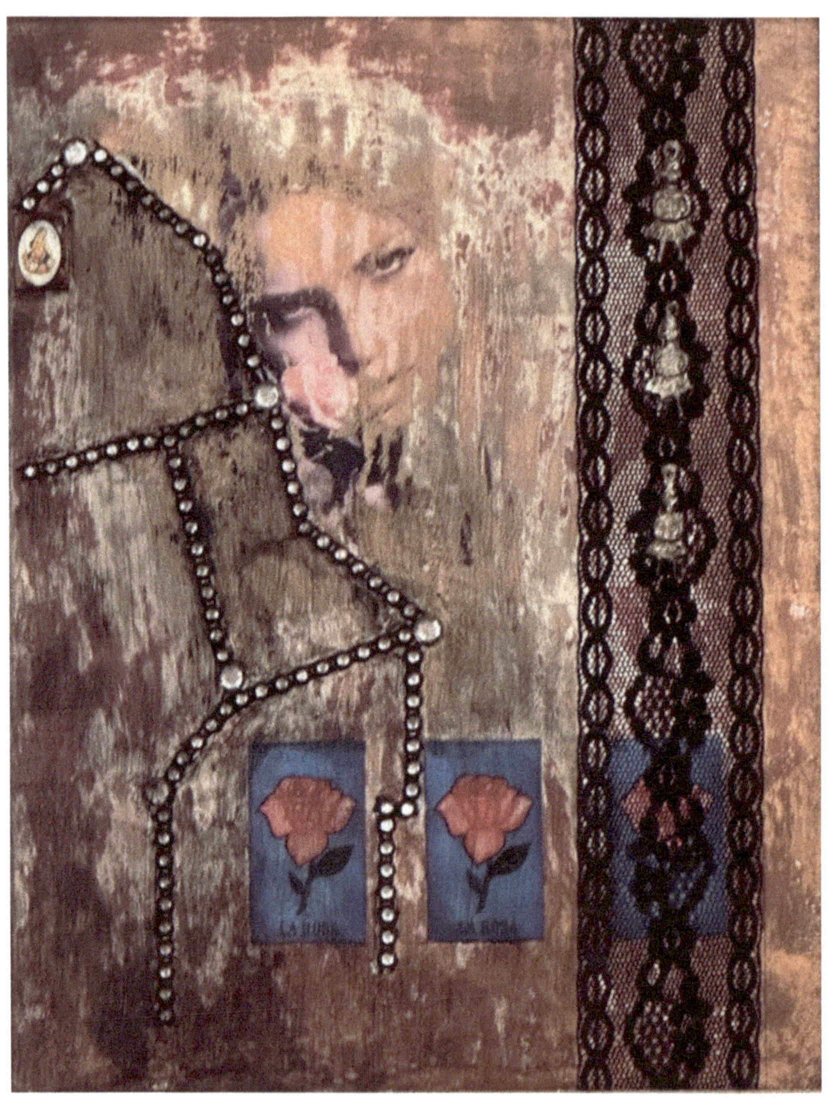

God's Promise of Glory

Away from the glowing city,
after a good meal of Belgian stew,
cuddled with three granddaughters,
resting in a meadow of tall fescue —
we share one pair of binoculars,
following stars like three wise astronomers.
Those twinkling numerous multitudes —
evangelions that glorify *Him who made*
the Pleiades and Orion.

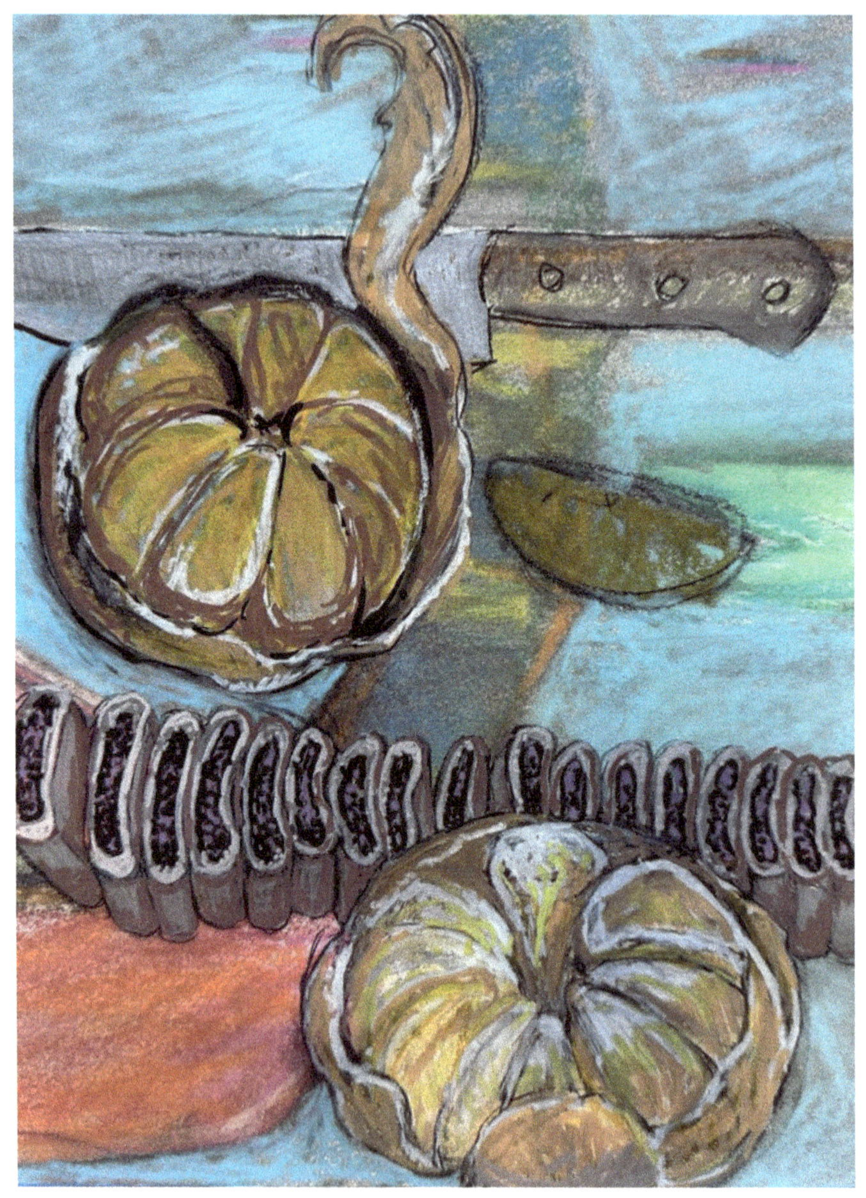

My Mother's Favorite Snack

Figs Newton's and oranges — their taste
a terse ripe complement.
The acidity of her bite — suitable
as the tart complex undertones
of figs and oranges —
not the engineered Bellas —
too easy, she'd say.

The hard work of knifing
through a thick roily rind,
then picking off — orange fingernails —
the spongy layer of pith pleases
the taste — the sweet spurt —
juicy flesh of the fruit.

The creased set of her mouth
exhales a spicy sigh when
a nibble combines the juice
with the crumbly cake-crust
of the wrapped gritty fig.

She chews words with a hint
of zest, pronounces judgements
filled with crunchy seeds.

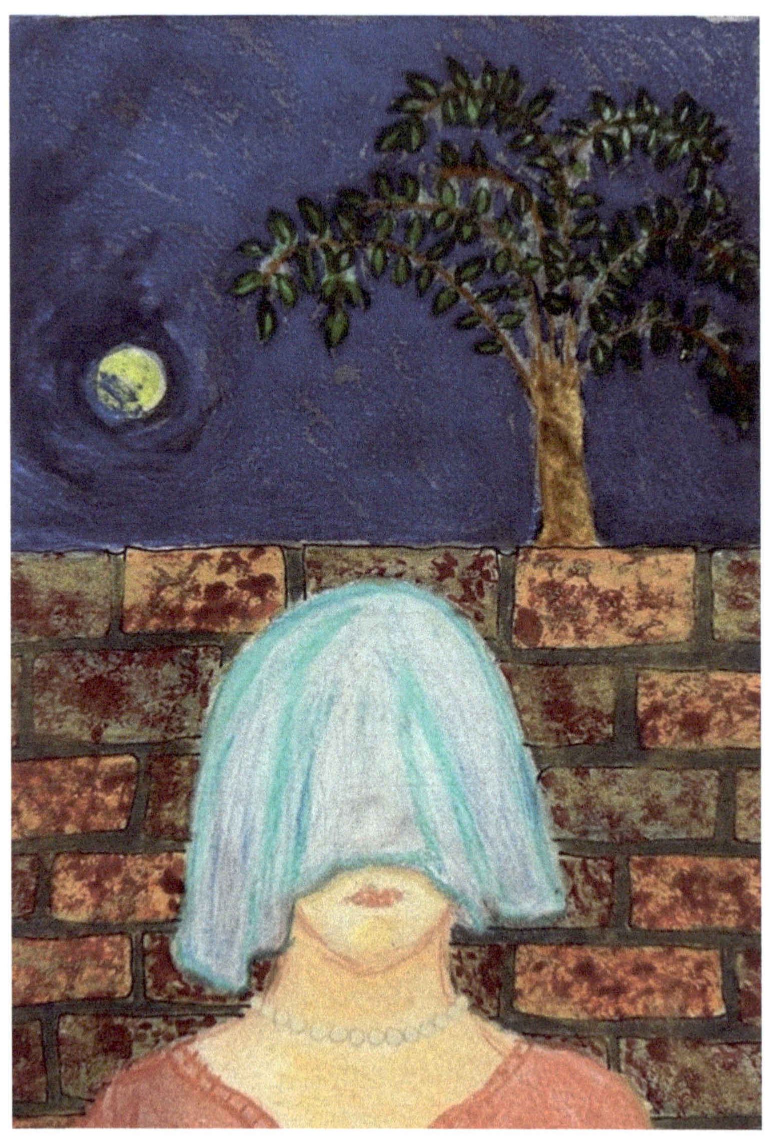

Hide and Seek

Mother smothers her head
under soft sky-blue flannel.
Surprise— NOW she blinks her eyes!

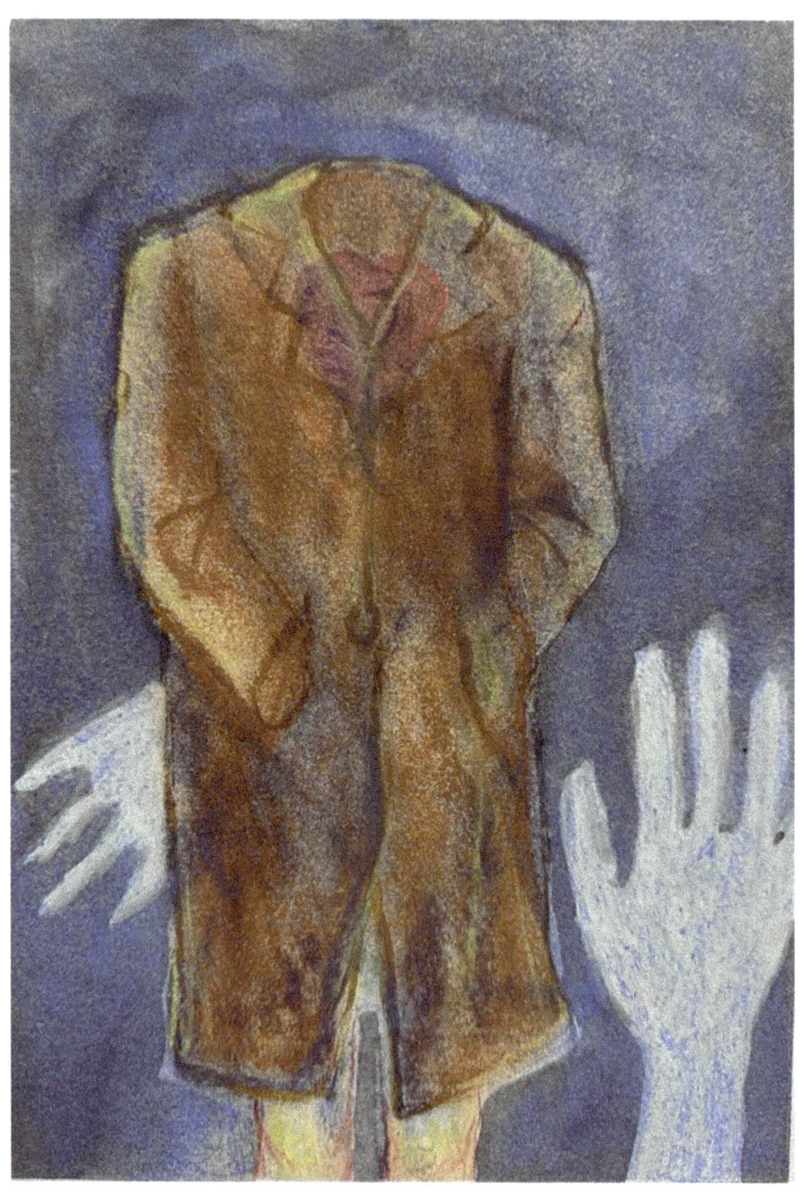

Warm woolen darkness smells so safe
yet your buried heart thrums in fear —
then chalky hands find YOU.

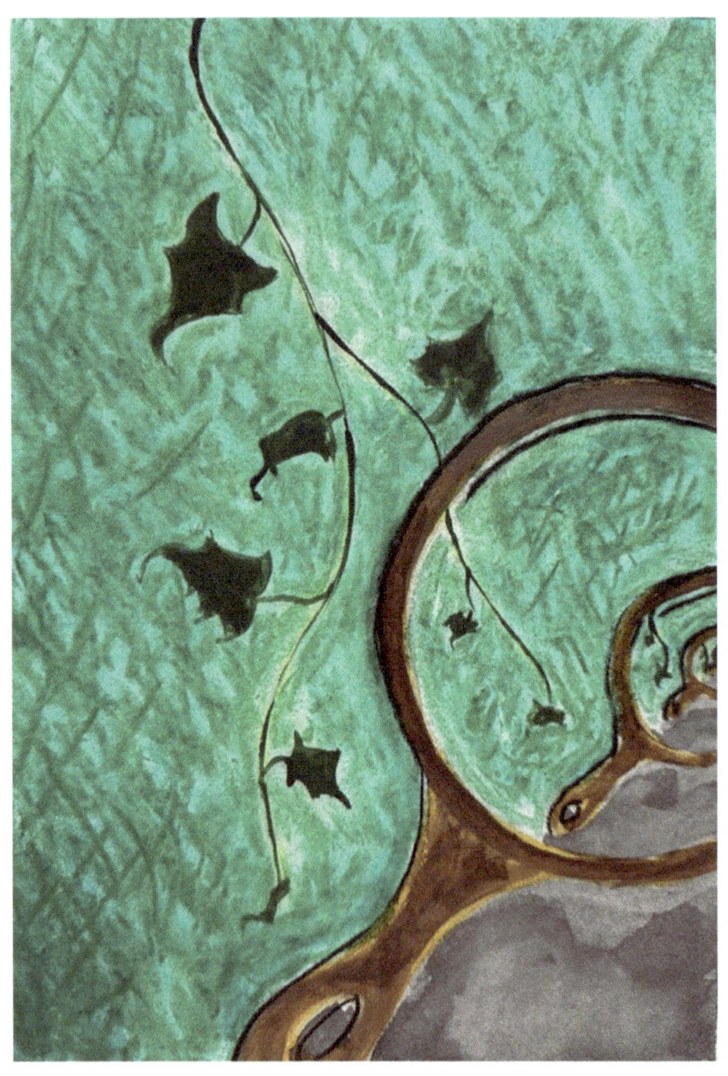

Blind mirrors only SEE themselves.

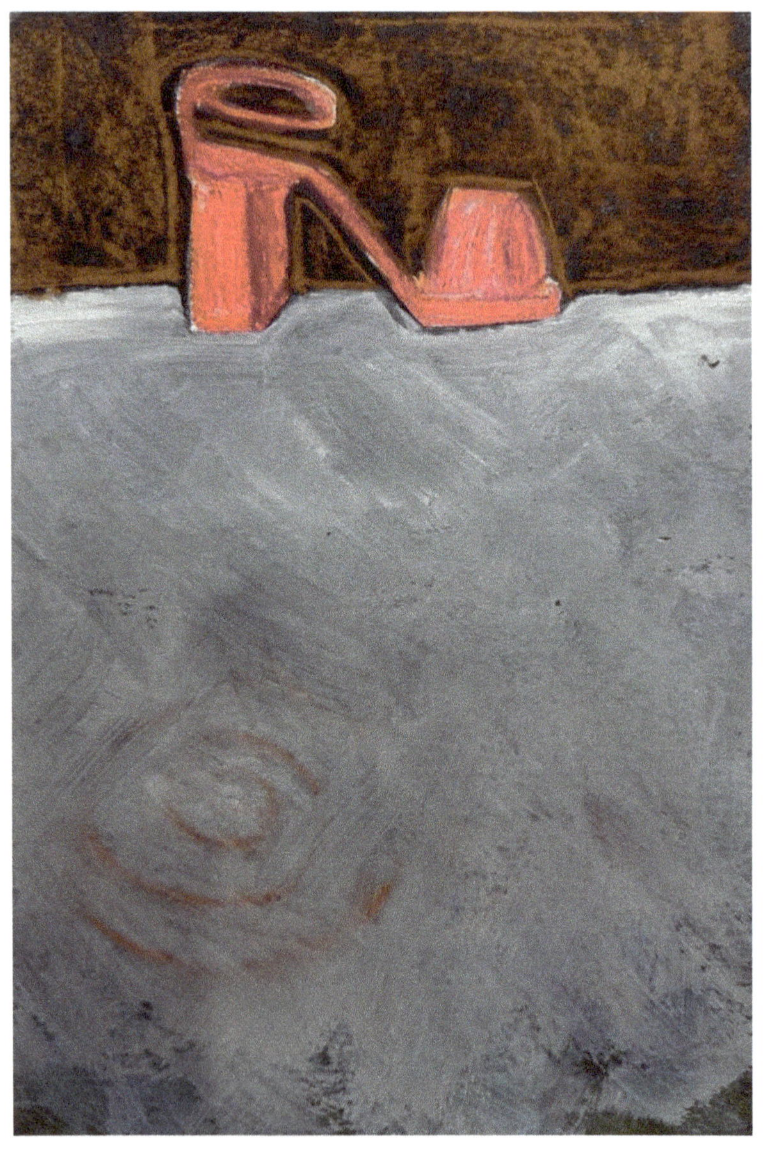

My bold red shoes steer ME
straight, deep into mascara cave
where paint obscures the rock face.

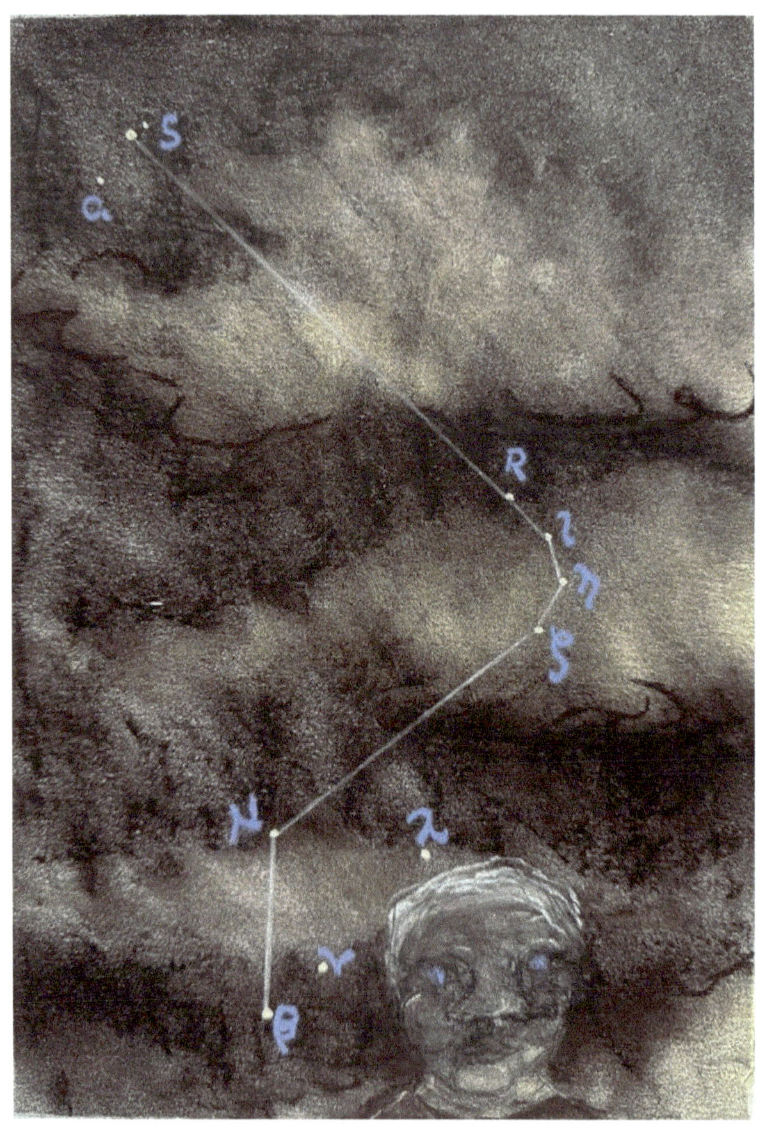

An old woman squints at the sky
and nods, NOW verifying
God's eyes are never visible
behind the stars.

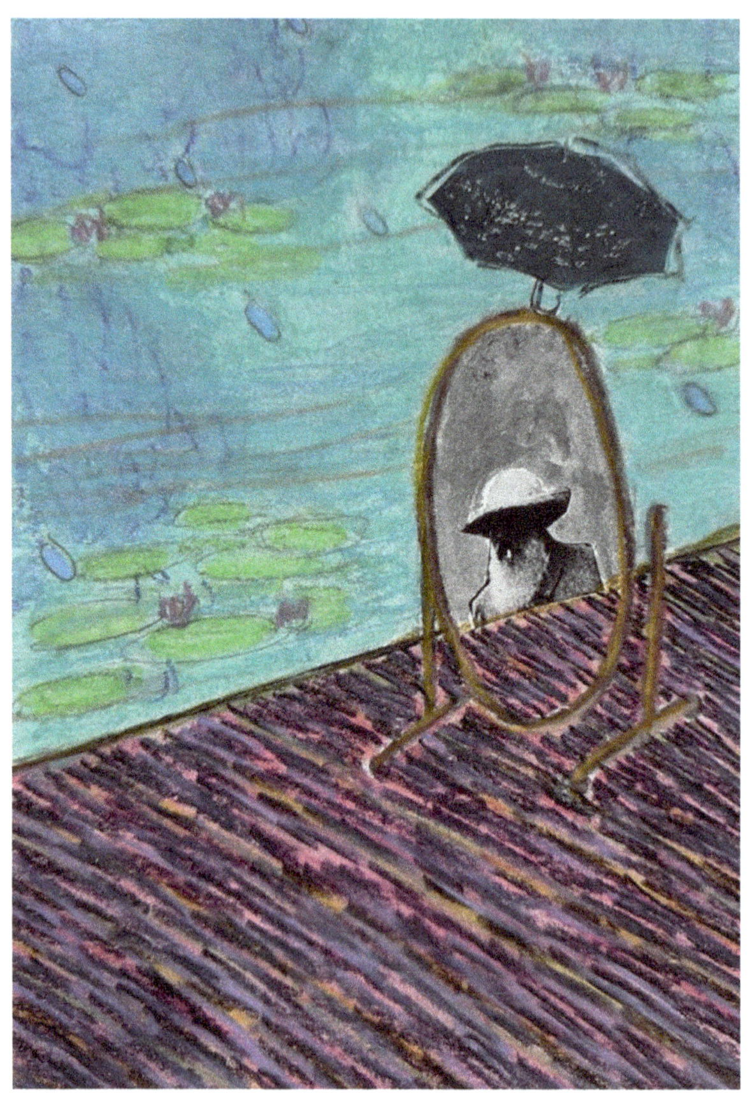

Honesty's reflection eludes YOU
when you DON'T own your story.

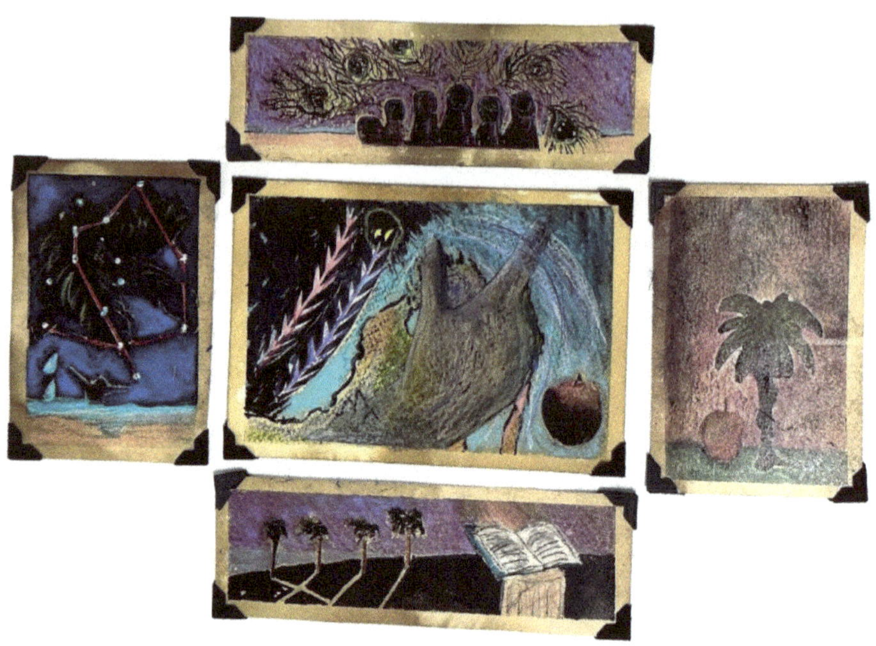

Postcard Promises

Dear Pavonis,
Here in paradise,
on the peninsula of Pélopenèse
apples plucked from palm trees,
if eaten,
proffer the pithy gift
of poriferous prophecy.
Should I attempt?
Love,
Persona

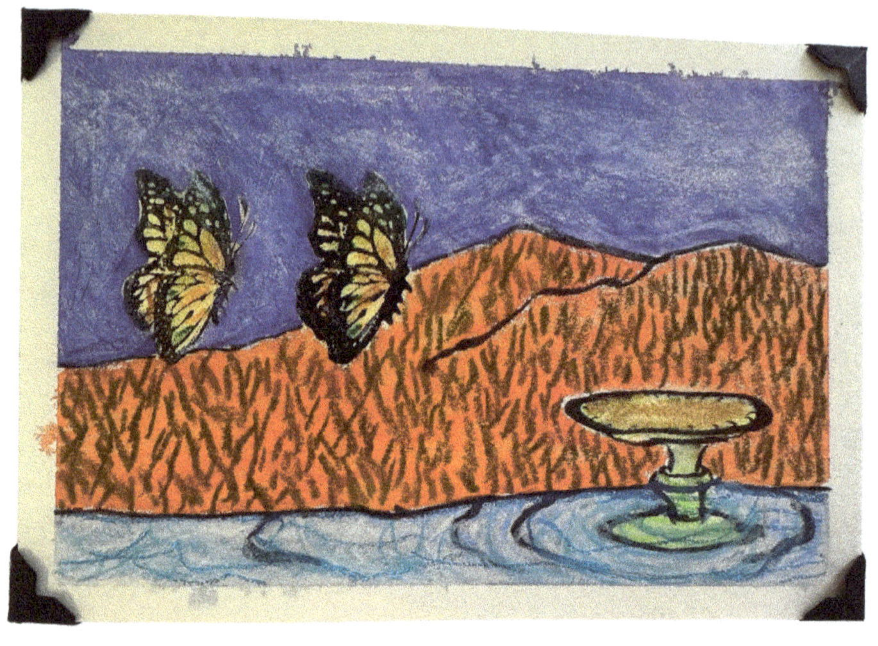

Dearest Martha,

Here in the mountains of Magyar,
mushrooms and monarchs whisper the egress
into the ears of Madonna Lily.

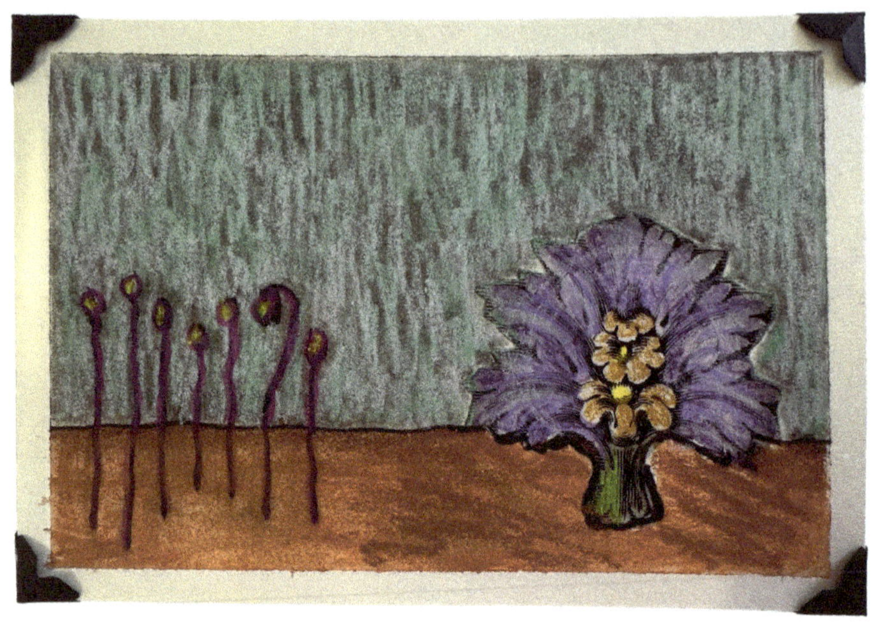

Do they screech
when you pluck
the ephemeral pubescent stamen
from the brow,
dictate their position
in the compote?

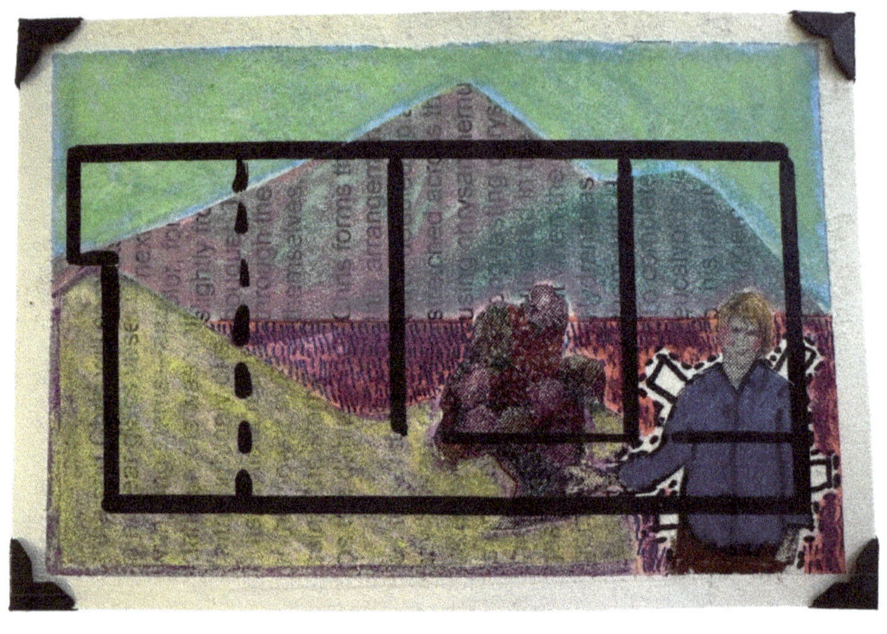

Thus picked,
the moonflower peeks
between fingers
on the knoll
riding the milkweed's wings.
Transfiguration sings
of vestal love,
echoing,
down empty halls
of your polished home.

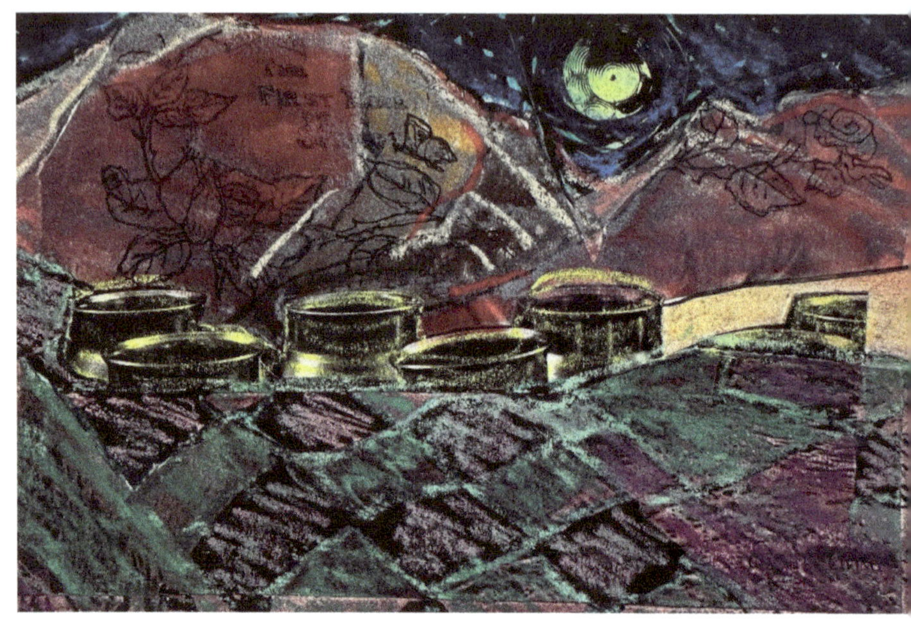

Carpathian's mount catches the echo,
crams the waves into rows of jars.

Martha,
Madonna and I crave
your expertise.

Unfeigned,
Mage

The Dancers

A treasured wedding gift from her long-dead
husband,
she wears the genuine pearl necklace
with comfortable grey sweatpants.
Shielding her body from chill
a purple sweater drapes her shoulders.
On her feet scuffed, torn ballet flats.

She shuffles in fear of falling flat,
remembering dancing on stage with her husband,
when he lifted her high on his shoulders,
her lithe body wrapped around his like a necklace
a dazzle which gave those watching a chill.
Now her breath an adagio of audible pants.

With a faint tremolo she grips her pants,
her mind vanishes, her eyes distant and flat.
Wrapped in the purple sweater stage-fighting the
reflective chill,
she shivers recalling her perished husband.
Then raising one hand, fingers with dolce the pearl
necklace
and sighing, she slowly pirouettes with hunched
shoulders.

Responding as her daughter touches her shoulder,
she returns to the present, her soul pants
breathing pearlescent like her necklace
and dances, twirls, then turns tombé flat.
She faces her daughter — so like her husband,
who guides her to the fireplace to remove the chill.

Agitated — her daughter reminds her to chill
demanding she sit and relax her shoulders.
Always in control, she thinks, like her principal
husband.
Then, nervously plucking the string on her pants,
she purposely contra-steps and rebels out flat
causing choreographic chaos — like knots in a
necklace.

Her daughter reaches over and smooths the
necklace,
she withdraws — only hearing an audience
cheering with chills
upon seeing her footwork and feats — not flat
but gracefully flying perfectly onto his shoulders.
With memory, excitement, and exertion she pants
dancing the grand Pas de Deux with her husband.

A manége of ballerinas like that pearl necklace
surrounds her husband
in arabesque, one foot flat with square shoulders.
Memories leave the chilled soul and settle deep
into the heart with sighs and breathy pants.

Made Perfect

Pickle spoon, weeping willow switch
and the father's leather belt which
quickly whipped off —
the punishment wrought
upon him makes us whole
and sculpts our worsted soul.

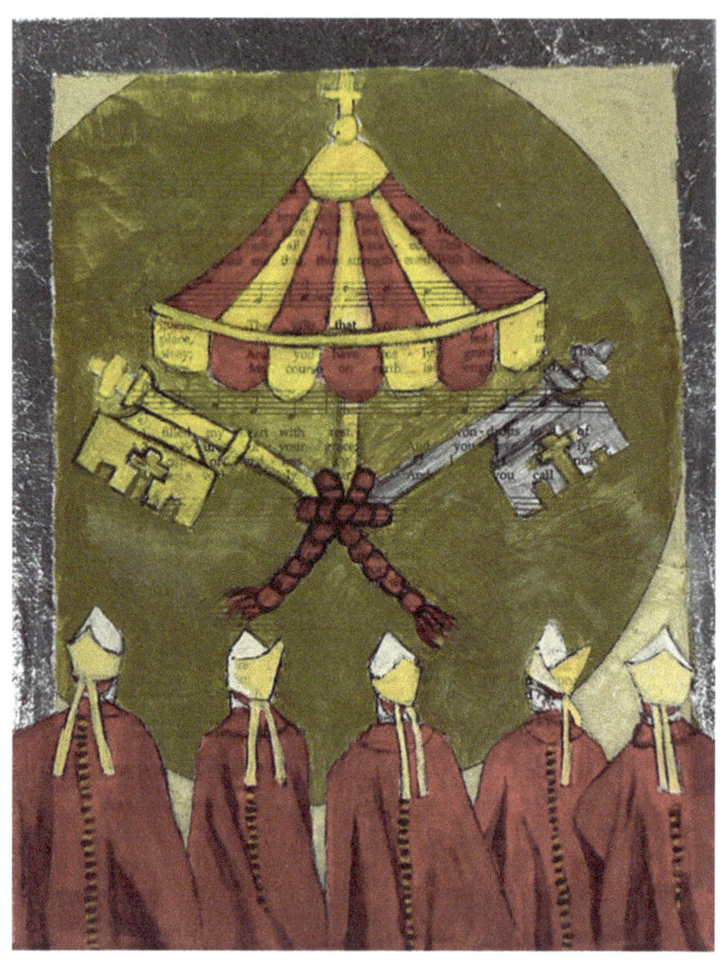
that
you
with
your
you
you call
of

Conclave

Blowing off
ecclesiastical dust
from the top of the frame.
Silver-leafed pontificate,
his photo replaced
with a red and yellow
striped umbrella.
The showmen praying
in the circular arena.
Rounds and rounds
and rounds of casting
keys strung on a rope.
Who will emerge
from The Big Top?

The Cooper Hawk's flight

no fanfare — with a quick stroke
lifts my eyes above.

Songbirds' hopeful play
at the start of a new day —
such plume, pluck, panache!

The bird's bustle, babble
stop in sudden-still silence
alert to His presence.

Magnify

A V of black-bellied ducks
fly low in dawn’s damp sky
their whistle of praise
magnifies my morning prayer.

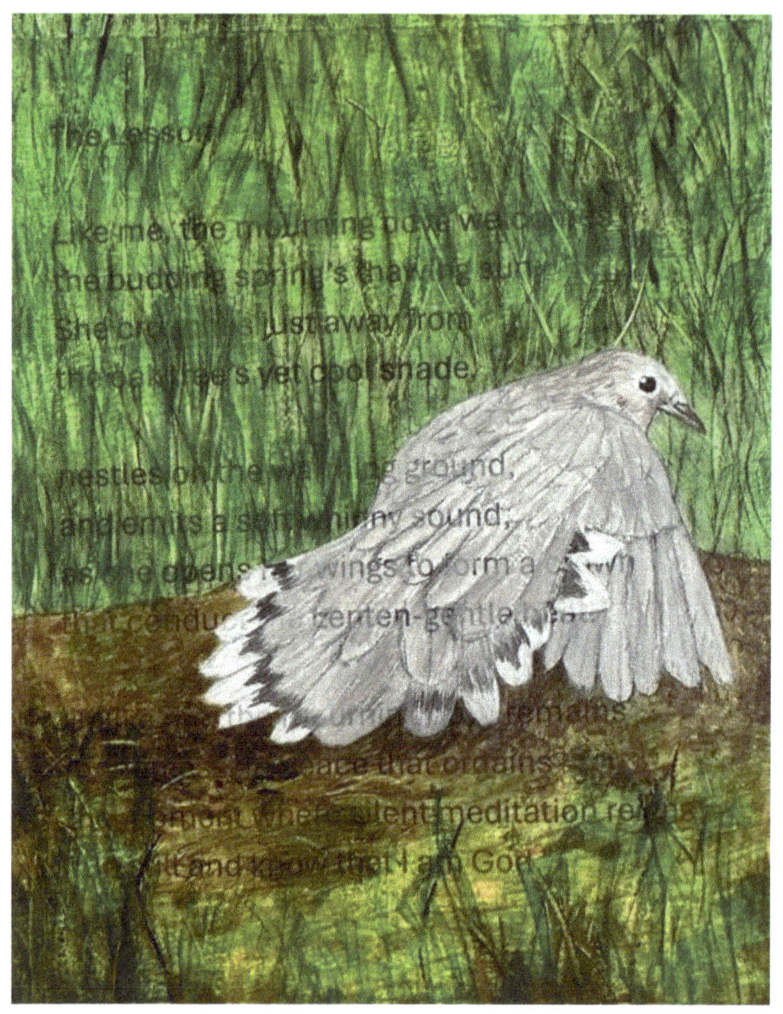
Like me, the
spring's
just away from
yet cool shade,
ground,
sound,
wings to form a
Lenten-gentle
remains
that ordains
meditation
and know that I am God

The Lesson

Like me, the mourning dove welcomes
the budding spring's thawing sun.
She crouches just away from
the oak tree's yet cool shade,

nestles on the warming ground,
and emits a soft sunny sound,
as she opens her wings to form a crown
that conducts the Lenten-gentle heat.

Unlike me, the mourning dove remains
motionless, in peace that ordains
the moment where silent meditation reigns.
Be still, and know that I am God!

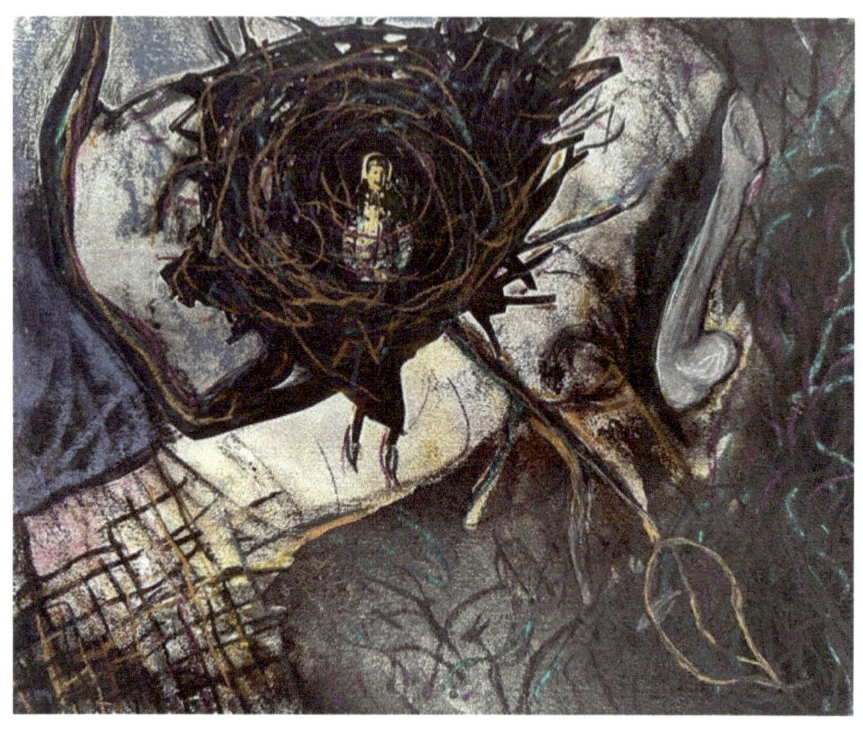

Emptiness

Remnants of a constructed nest
within the arms of the chandelier rest.

Hanging over the pitched porch portent
the cradle of sticks laments.

The forte of mother wren's dirge
notes directed to God of pain's scourge.

Warble-whips of loss and emptiness
bound, tangled rute dislodged from her breast.

Quiverings of Gethsemane
repeat the Savior's song — the beating way

is the timbre, freeing us from distress
within glad arms of perfect rest.

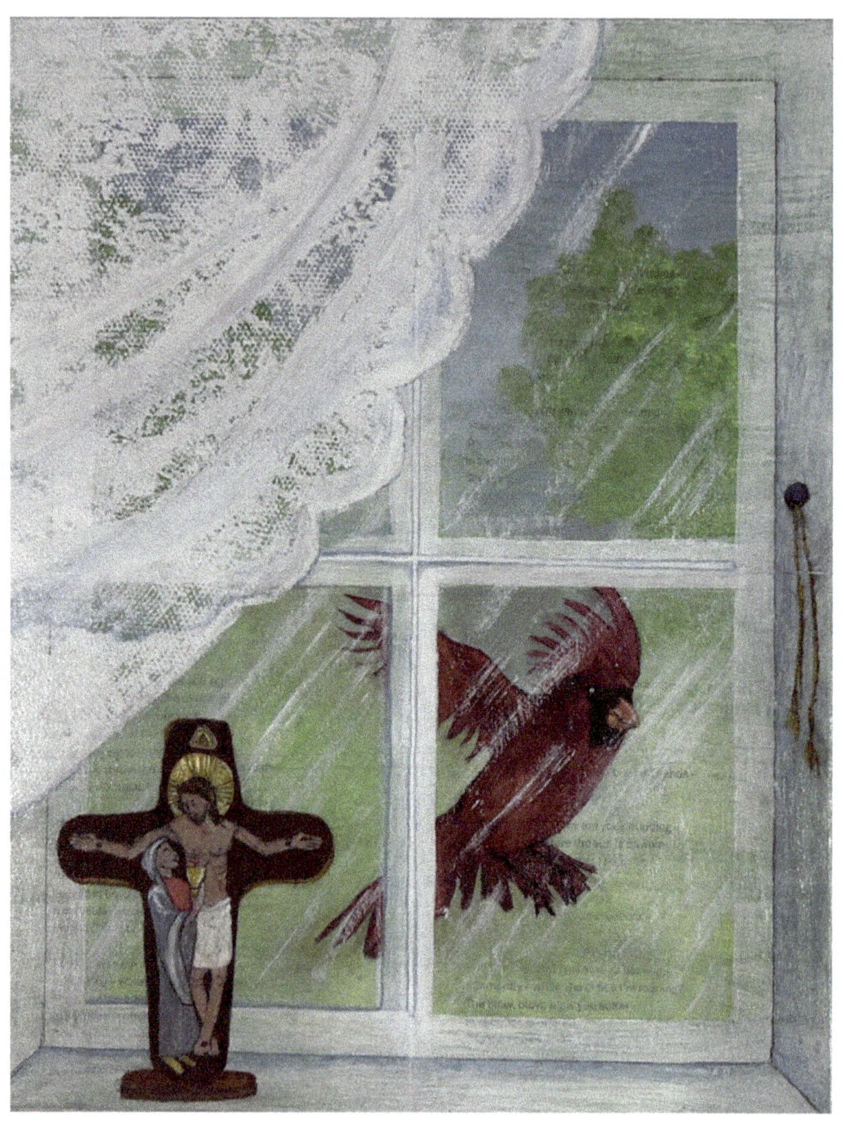

Easter Call

Red bird, red bird why are you knocking —
insistently — so early this morning?
The rap, rap, rap of your wings
like the sound of the hammer pings,
nailing my savior to the tree.
my ropes of sin freed.

Red bird, red bird why are you pounding —
tenaciously — before the sun is dawning?
The thud, thud, thud that I hear
moved by love beyond fear
flogged in body he persists—
my gall untwists.

Red bird, red bird why are you beating —
adamantly — while The Office I'm reading?
The blow, blow, blow you suffer
in sacrifice is offered.
See the marks of his passion—
my image refashioned.

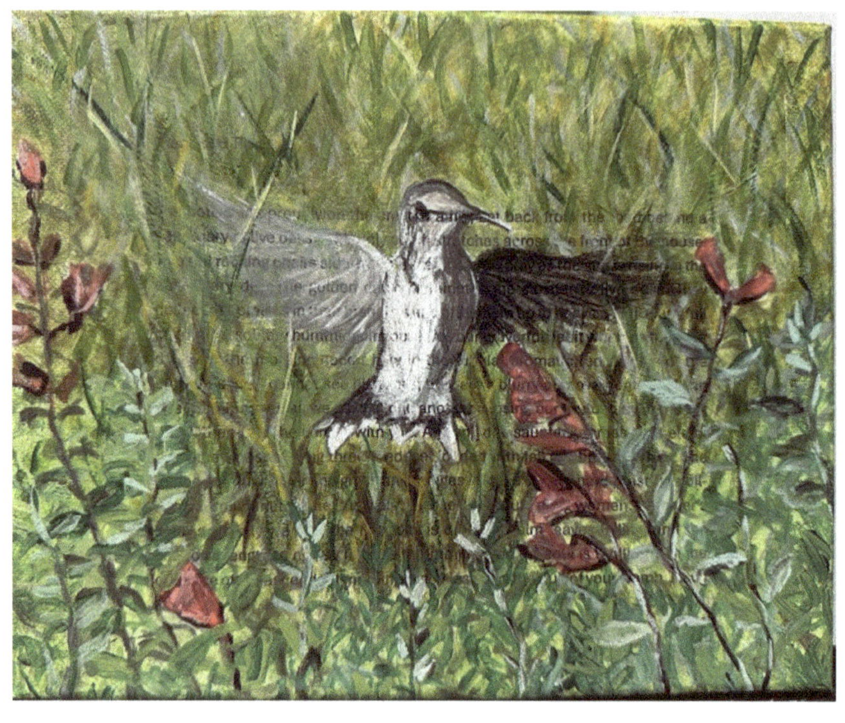

Morning Prayer on the Porch

The house sits proudly on the crest of a hill, set back from the road behind a sanctuary of live oaks. A friendly porch stretches across its front. Two red rocking chairs side-by-side are where we daily pray as the sun rises. The golden dawn illuminates the cloister of live oaks, collects our praises in their branches and offers them to heaven. *Hail Mary, full of grace.* A solitary hummingbird observes our prayerful habit when he fuels his day with the morning nectar held in the tubular aromatic red flowers of the autumn sage. I cannot see his wings—they are a blurry of movement—but we gaze at one another with mutual joy for the gift of another day. *The Lord is with you.* A young doe saunters across the field of tall turkey grass waving three-toed feet loaded with fall red-bronze seeds. She forgoes drying grass and forages instead for the hard mast—the oil-rich acorns buried in the dusty dirt. *Blessed are you among women.* Summer's heat is slightly waning, humidity is dropping, elm leaves falling, shadows lengthening. My heart is thrumming, and my soul is thrilling with the cadence of the ascendent morning. *And blessed is the fruit of your womb, Jesus.* Amen.

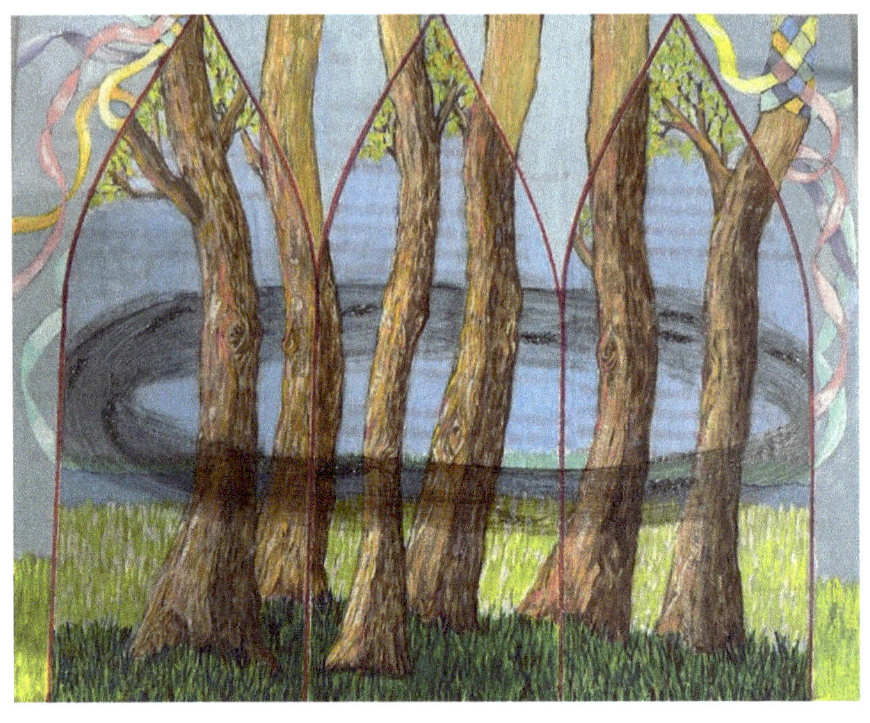

Starlings in Texas

Who are these that fly like a cloud,
as they whirl and dance with fury —
their flap of wings a blurred flurry,
black feathers with shining stars bowed?

A beautiful madness of unity,
they encircle a cloister of six oaks
plaiting invisible ribbons of hopes —
the Spirit's tether entwined perfectly.

Then, mysteriously they turn as one,
a silent listening guiding their flight —
lengthening streamers of promises bright
unwinding my anxious thoughts so well spun.

Mary Oliver wants wings — to be improbable
Behold, *for nothing will be impossible with God.*

Scripture Notes

Page 43, “My Granddaughters Named It Anselm” – Isaiah 61:3b (New Revised Standard Version-Catholic Edition, NRSVCE)

Page 45, “Willing to Become” – Psalm 22:14; Isaiah 38:13 (NRSVCE)

Page 47, "A Thistle Tumbling” – Psalm 83:13 (NRSVCE)

Page 53, “Redeemed” – Inspired by Psalm 50:11; Jeremiah 31:15 (NRSVCE)

Page 57, “God’s Promise of Glory” – Amos 5:8a (NRSVCE)

Page 91, "The Lesson” – Psalm 46:10 (NRSVCE)

Page 99, "Starlings in Texas” – Isaiah 60:8; Luke 1:37 (NRSVCE)

www.ingramcontent.com/pod-product-compliance
Lightning Source LLC
LaVergne TN
LVHW060933110826
845147LV00029B/773

* 9 7 9 8 2 1 8 9 1 8 0 7 1 *